BASEBALL SMARTS

WHAT DOES A PITCHER DO?

Paul Challen

PowerKiDS press

New York

Published in 2017 by The Rosen Publishing Group, Inc.
29 East 21st Street, New York, NY 10010

Cataloging-in-Publication Data
Names: Challen, Paul.
Title: What does a pitcher do? / Paul Challen.
Description: New York : PowerKids Press, 2017. | Series: Baseball smarts | Includes index.
Identifiers: ISBN 9781499432893 (pbk.) | ISBN 9781499432916 (library bound) |
  ISBN 9781499432909 (6 pack)
Subjects: LCSH: Pitching (Baseball)--Juvenile literature.Pitchers (Baseball)--Juvenile literature.
Classification: LCC GV871.C53 2017 | DDC 796.357'22--dc23

Developed and Produced for Rosen by BlueAppleWorks Inc.
Managing Editor for BlueAppleWorks: Melissa McClellan
Art Director: Tibor Choleva
Designer: Joshua Avramson
Photo Research: Jane Reid
Editor: Marcia Abramson

Photo Credits: Cover left Peter Weber/Shutterstock; cover right Fuse/Thinkstock; page tops Photology1971/Shutterstock; title page middle cthomas888/iStockphoto; page bottoms lasha/Shutterstock; TOC David Lee/Shutterstock; page backgrounds bottom Shawn Zhang /Shutterstock; page backgrounds top, p. 4, p. 7 left Eric Broder Van Dyke/Shutterstock; p. 5 Ffooter/ Shutterstock; p. 6 left, 6 right Arturo Pardavila III/Creative Commons; p. 7 right Aspenphoto/Dreamstime.com; p. 8 Eric Broder Van Dyke/Dreamstime.com; p. 9 Photographerlondon/Dreamstime.com; p. 10 Peter Weber/Shutterstock; p. 11 Alan Crosthwaite/ Dreamstime.com; p. 12 left Spectruminfo/Dreamstime.com; p. 12 right, 19, 29 top Aspen Photo/Shutterstock.com; p. 13, 16, 24, 25, 26 left, 27 top Jerry Coli/Dreamstime.com; p. 14 Debby Wong/Shutterstock.com; p. 15 Bill Florence/Shutterstock.com; p. 17 Jupiterimages/Thinkstock; p. 18 Paparazzofamily/Dreamstime.com; p. 20 Rtrembly/Dreamstime.com; p. 21 Flair Images/ Dreamstime.com; p. 22 © Jose Luis Villegas/Keystone Press; p. 23, 26 left Scott Anderson/Dreamstime.com; p. 27 left LiAnna Davis/Creative Commons; p. 27 right Arturo Pardavila III/Creative Commons; p. 28 Americanspirit/Dreamstime.com; p. 29 Susan Leggett/Dreamstime.com; back cover Eugene Onischenko/Shutterstock

Manufactured in the United States of America
CPSIA Compliance Information: Batch #BW17PK For Further Information contact: Rosen Publishing, New York, New York at 1-800-237-9932

CONTENTS

THE BASEBALL TEAM

Two teams go head-to-head in the exciting sport of baseball. Each team fields nine players, and the games are divided into innings. Each inning, the teams switch between offense and defense. The team on the offensive side tries to hit the ball and score runs. On the defensive side, the team tries to stop the opponents from hitting and scoring by using their skill in pitching, catching, and throwing.

The defensive side of a team is made up of a pitcher, infielders, outfielders, and a catcher. The pitcher and catcher work as a unit to try to strike out batters, or force them to hit balls that are easy to catch. The infielders are the closest players to home plate. They try to field hit balls that come their way. Outfielders are the farthest away from home plate and try to catch long balls hit to them.

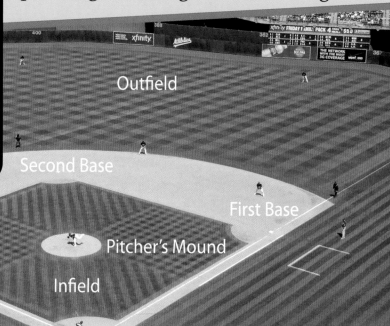

Outfield

Second Base

First Base

Third Base

Pitcher's Mound

Infield

Home Plate

THE BASEBALL BATTERY

The pitcher and the catcher combine to make up what baseball fans call the **battery**. The pitcher stands on the pitcher's **mound**, a raised part of the field that is 60 feet, 6 inches (18.4 m) from home plate. The catcher crouches behind home plate to try to catch the pitcher's pitches. In between these two defensive players stands the batter, who tries to hit the pitches coming from the mound.

Pitchers use all kinds of spins on the ball to make it move in different ways. Skilled pitchers can make a ball curve or drop to try to trick a hitter. Others use the fastball pitch as a way of overpowering a hitter.

Communication between the pitcher and catcher is key. Catchers use all kinds of finger signals to tell pitchers how to deliver the ball to home plate.

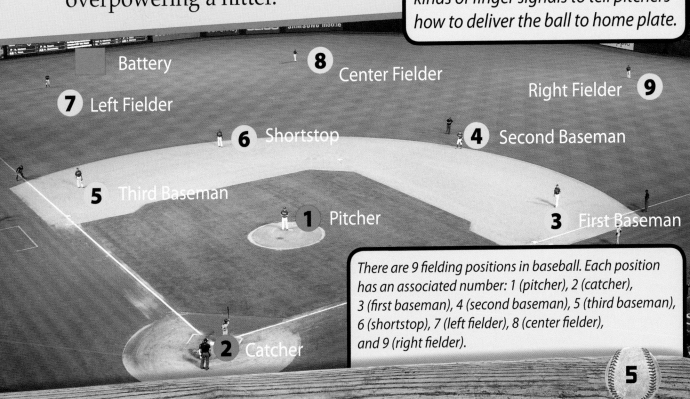

Battery

8 Center Fielder

Right Fielder **9**

7 Left Fielder

6 Shortstop

4 Second Baseman

5 Third Baseman

1 Pitcher

3 First Baseman

There are 9 fielding positions in baseball. Each position has an associated number: 1 (pitcher), 2 (catcher), 3 (first baseman), 4 (second baseman), 5 (third baseman), 6 (shortstop), 7 (left fielder), 8 (center fielder), and 9 (right fielder).

2 Catcher

THE PITCH

The pitchers can normally be divided into three roles: the starting **rotation**, the middle-relief, and the late-innings **relievers**. The middle-relief and late-innings relievers form what is known as the **bullpen**. The two best pitchers on a team are known as the **ace** and the **closer**. The ace is the best starting pitcher and the closer is the best reliever.

Pitchers come in all sizes. Kansas City Royals **starter** Chris Young (left) stands 6-foot-10 (2 m) while Marcus Stroman of the Toronto Blue Jays is 5-foot-8 (1.7 m). On average, though, pitchers have been getting taller, and height is considered an advantage.

DID YOU KNOW?

Baseball pitchers always strive for a "1-2-3" inning. That means that they retire all three batters in an inning without allowing any of them to get to first base. This can be done via strikeouts or by the batters hitting into outs, such as a fly ball being caught, or ground balls being fielded and thrown to first before the batter can run there. It is possible to retire all three batters on three pitches.

Each play starts when the pitcher throws the ball to the catcher behind home plate. Top pitchers need to be smart baseball thinkers as well as good athletes. Professional pitchers, with the help of their teammates and coaches, will prepare for every hitter they are going to face in a game.

A pitcher throws from the top of the pitching mound in the center of the baseball infield.

7

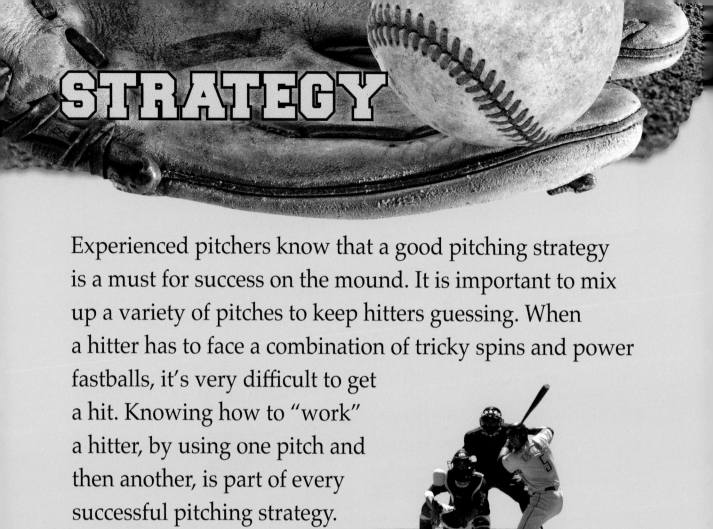

STRATEGY

Experienced pitchers know that a good pitching strategy is a must for success on the mound. It is important to mix up a variety of pitches to keep hitters guessing. When a hitter has to face a combination of tricky spins and power fastballs, it's very difficult to get a hit. Knowing how to "work" a hitter, by using one pitch and then another, is part of every successful pitching strategy.

Pitchers will also have done their homework to determine what kind of pitches each hitter hates facing – and of course they try to throw those whenever they can.

PITCH PERFECT

Pitchers need to be able to throw pitches accurately. Being able to locate pitches where you want to throw them leads to confidence when facing batters. A pitcher with good control knows that no matter who the hitter is, it will be possible to deliver a pitch to the hitter's weak spot most of the time.

Once pitchers master control, they can work on velocity—that is, the speed of the pitch. Most pitchers agree that there is not much point being able to throw hard unless your pitches are also accurate. Of course, being able to combine both control and velocity is the aim of all pitchers—but it takes a lot of practice and coaching to be able to do it.

The mental part of pitching is just as important as the physical part. It takes great concentration and the ability to outthink a hitter to succeed on the mound. Most great pitchers are also excellent baseball strategists who understand how to get hitters out.

THE RIGHT STANCE

Pitchers can use two basic stances when getting ready to pitch. The first of these is the windup. This is the more complicated of the two stances, but can allow the pitcher to deliver the ball with great speed and power. Using the windup, the pitcher faces the batter, rears back, and takes a small step back with the foot opposite to the pitching hand. The pitcher then makes a slight turn with the opposite shoulder facing home plate. The pitcher's opposite leg rises up and then strides forward towards home plate as the ball is delivered to the catcher.

As well as a good stance, pitchers need good mechanics when they throw.

Pitchers who use the stretch motion can get more control of their pitches. This stance is used more often when runners are on base, since it takes less time than the windup to deliver to home plate, making it harder for runners to steal bases. In the stretch, the pitcher stands at an angle with both feet pointed towards third base (for right-handed pitchers) or first base (for left-handers). The pitcher raises the opposite leg to the pitching arm, rotates the body slightly, and strides towards home with a slight knee lift while delivering the ball to the catcher.

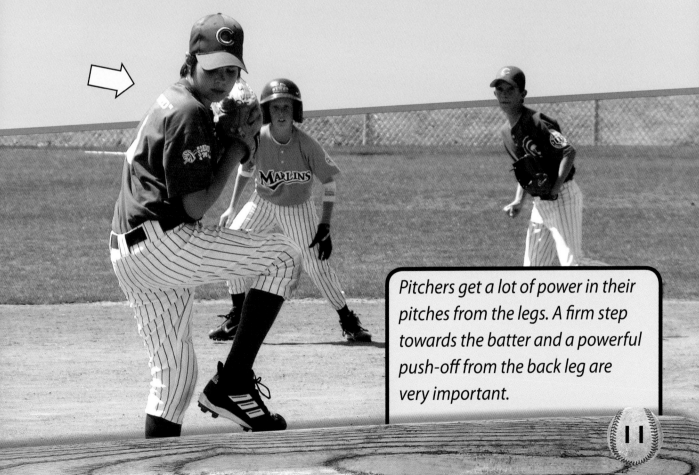

Pitchers get a lot of power in their pitches from the legs. A firm step towards the batter and a powerful push-off from the back leg are very important.

PITCH SELECTION

A pitcher can use several pitches to try to get batters out. The secret to throwing different types of pitches lies in how the pitcher grips the ball, and what kind of spin these special grips put on a pitch. One of the most common is the fastball. To throw a two-seam fastball, the pitcher holds the ball with fingers placed along the seams of the ball and the thumb at the back of the ball. This pitch tends to travel fairly straight towards the batter and—as the name suggests—has a lot of speed.

To throw a simple curve ball, the ball is gripped with the middle finger along the bottom seam and the thumb on the back seam. This grip gives the ball spin that puts a curve on the pitch and can be very confusing to a batter.

TRICKY PITCHES

The change-up is one of the most confusing pitches for a hitter. The pitcher disguises this one to look like a fastball, and the hitter expects it will be coming in with the same speed and rotation as a very fast pitch. But the skilled change-up pitcher will take some of the velocity off the change-up, and with a slightly different grip and arm motion will try to throw off a hitter's swing.

One famous pitch—the knuckleball—is actually thrown with no or very little spin at all. The aim here is for air currents inside a stadium to cause the ball to dip and drop in ways that are very confusing to a batter.

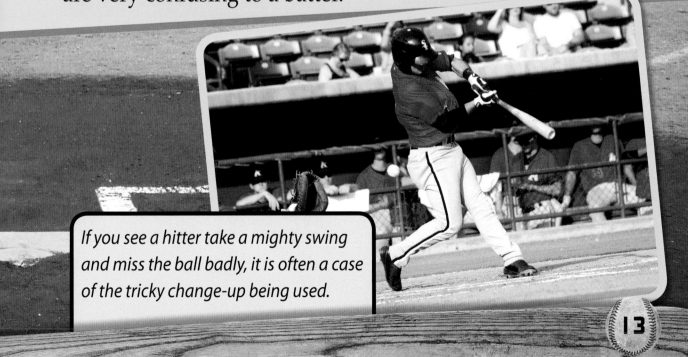

If you see a hitter take a mighty swing and miss the ball badly, it is often a case of the tricky change-up being used.

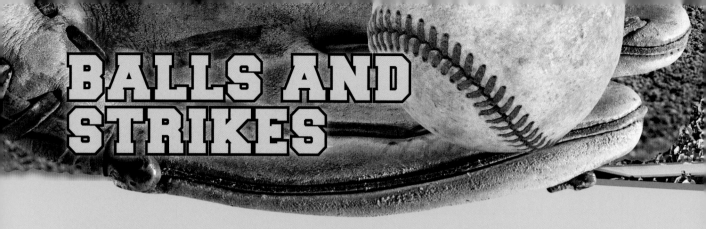

BALLS AND STRIKES

The key to good pitching is knowing the difference between balls and strikes. Any pitch that a hitter swings at and misses will be called a strike by the umpire. After three strikes the batter is called "out." A **foul ball** will be called either the first or second strike—but you cannot strike out on a foul ball. If a batter does not swing at a pitch, it can still be called a strike by the umpire if it crosses home plate within the strike zone.

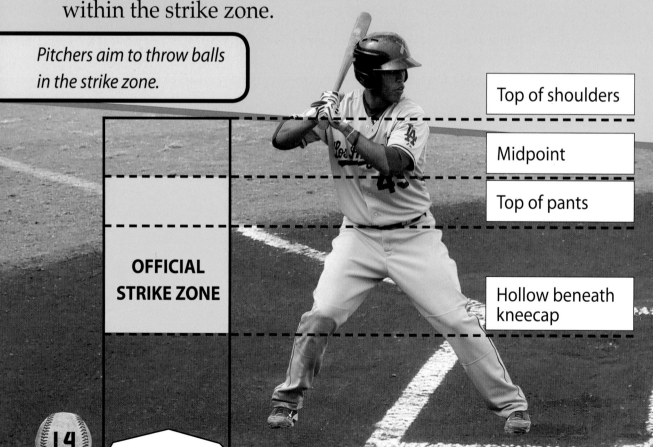

Pitchers aim to throw balls in the strike zone.

Top of shoulders

Midpoint

Top of pants

Hollow beneath kneecap

OFFICIAL STRIKE ZONE

DID YOU KNOW?

In baseball, the "count" refers to the number of balls and strikes a batter has. Balls are always mentioned first, so a "1-2 count" means a batter has one ball and two strikes. A "full count" is 3-2. Pitchers try to get "ahead in the count," which means a batter has more strikes than balls. This makes it easier for the pitcher to try riskier pitches in the hope of striking the batter out.

Any pitch that the hitter does not swing at or make contact with that crosses the plate outside the strike zone is called a ball by the umpire. After four balls, a batter gets a walk and is allowed to go to first base. Of course, pitchers try to throw more strikes than balls, but there are times when a pitcher will intentionally walk a hitter as part of a team's strategy. For example, if a team has already recorded two outs, it may make sense to walk a very strong hitter if a weaker batter is up next.

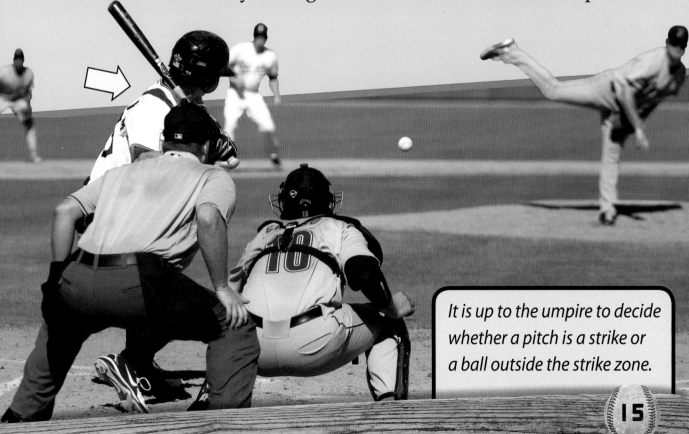

It is up to the umpire to decide whether a pitch is a strike or a ball outside the strike zone.

15

LOW AND HIGH BALL PITCHERS

Although every pitcher wants to strike out as many batters as possible, getting batters to hit the ball where it can be easily fielded is also a good defensive strategy. Players known as ground ball pitchers are experts at throwing the kinds of pitches that are often hit on the ground. They rely on their teammates in the infield to scoop up these grounders and throw them to the correct base for the out.

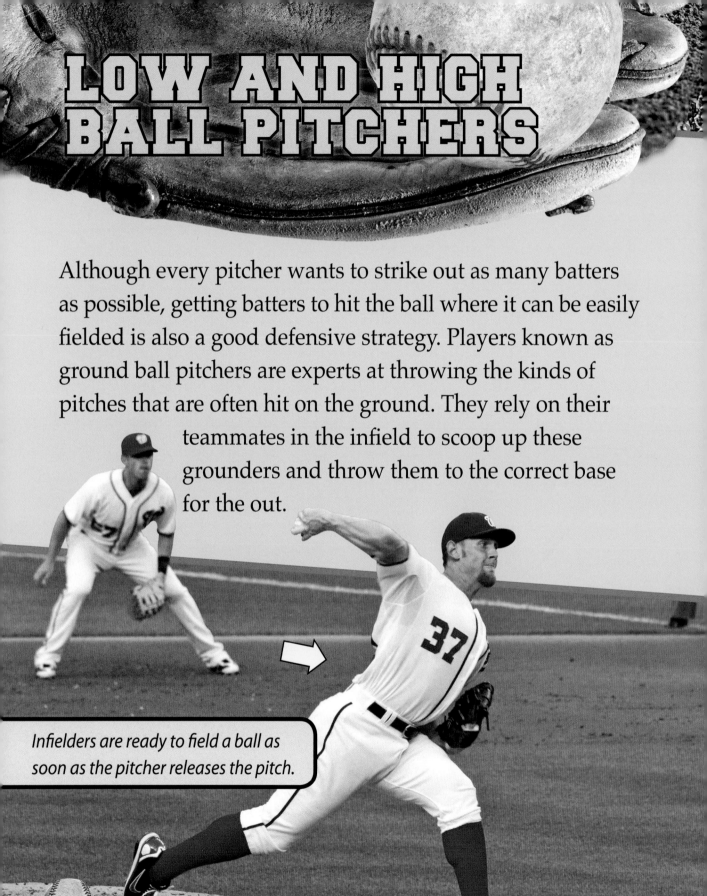

Infielders are ready to field a ball as soon as the pitcher releases the pitch.

UP IN THE AIR

Some pitchers try to get batters to hit balls high in the air with their **pitch selection**. These pitchers, known as fly ball pitchers, are confident that their teammates in the infield and outfield can get under these hit balls and catch them for an easy out. It takes coordination on a team to do this, and an understanding of where batters like to hit fly balls so that the fielders can get in good positions before the ball is hit.

Fly ball pitching can be risky, though. If a pitcher is just slightly off in controlling a pitch, there is always the chance that, instead of hitting a fly ball that is easy to catch, the batter can hit the ball for an extra-base hit and even a home run.

Pitchers always need to be aware of any runners who are on base. Often, a runner will try to steal a base. If pitchers see this in time, they can try to throw to a teammate covering that base to try to get the runner out. Catchers can also try to throw base runners out after catching a ball or strike at home plate.

Because it takes less time to throw to home plate from the stretch position, pitchers almost always use this approach when runners are on base.

Runners are out if they go too far from a base and the pitcher rifles the ball back to the fielder, who tags the runner before they get back. This move, called a pickoff, is easier to do from the stretch position.

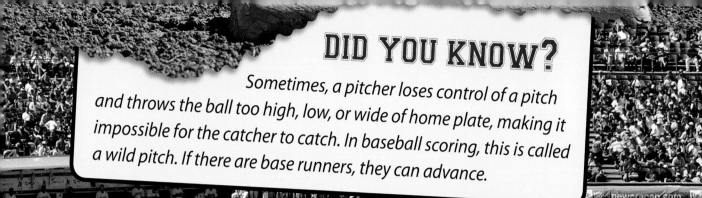

DID YOU KNOW?

Sometimes, a pitcher loses control of a pitch and throws the ball too high, low, or wide of home plate, making it impossible for the catcher to catch. In baseball scoring, this is called a wild pitch. If there are base runners, they can advance.

THE DOUBLE PLAY

A double play is any defensive play that results in two offensive players being called out. Many double plays happen when there is a runner on first. The shortstop or second baseman scoops up a grounder and throws it to the player covering second. That player will step on second to force out the runner coming from first, and then quickly throw to first. If the first baseman catches the ball with one foot on the bag before the runner arrives, it's a double play.

A double play is sometimes known as a pitcher's best friend, because it helps to bail a pitcher out of a jam.

WARMING UP

Since each play in a baseball game starts with a pitch, pitchers have a very demanding job. Always part of the action, they have to throw hard and accurately on every play. That is why it is absolutely crucial that a pitcher does a good warm-up before making the first pitch in a game. Warming up properly gets the pitching arm, as well as the legs, back and shoulders, ready for game action. Failing to have a good warm-up can lead to injury.

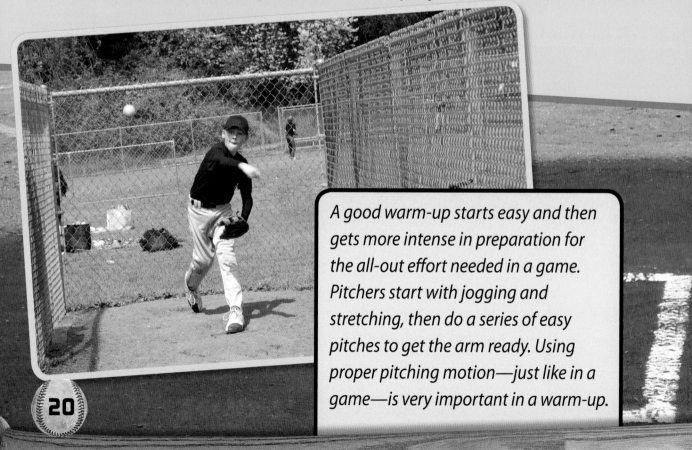

A good warm-up starts easy and then gets more intense in preparation for the all-out effort needed in a game. Pitchers start with jogging and stretching, then do a series of easy pitches to get the arm ready. Using proper pitching motion—just like in a game—is very important in a warm-up.

ON THE BENCH

Pitchers take long breaks from the action when they are not on the mound. While on the bench, it is important for pitchers to recover, so they can be ready to get back to pitching feeling fresh. There are a number of things a pitcher can do to help recovery. Pitchers often wrap their pitching arms in towels to keep them warm, or at least put on a jacket to keep the muscles warm.

It is also important to follow the game from the bench even when a pitcher is not playing. The hitters a pitcher will be facing in the field may give away small clues in their defensive play that could be helpful to a pitcher when they are batting.

Pitchers don't play every game because their job is so hard, but they can and should encourage their teammates from the bench.

HITTING THE BALL

Because they do such an important job on the defensive side of the game, pitchers are not usually expected to be great hitters. At the very least, a pitcher should be able to bunt to advance a runner if a player is on first base.

Since pitchers know the strike zone well from their position on the mound, many are able to be good judges of it when they are at bat. It is very rare in the professional game for a pitcher to be a home-run power hitter, but some have been good contact hitters.

*Madison Bumgarner of the San Francisco Giants is the rare pitcher who can hit home runs. Though he pitches left-handed, he hits right-handed. He hits so well that he was used as a **pinch hitter** in July 2016 and came through with a double!*

BUNTING

One way a batter can get on base is by bunting, and many pitchers use this approach when at the plate. Instead of swinging fully at the ball when it is pitched, bunting involves holding the bat out and letting the ball hit it. Rather than traveling a great distance, a good bunt will make the ball "go dead" and only take a short roll.

When this happens, the infielders, pitcher, and catcher all scramble to pick up the ball and throw it to first. As this is happening, a speedy runner can try to beat the throw and get to first base safely.

On a sacrifice bunt, the hitter will be thrown out at first, but teammates on other bases will be able to advance safely. The bunter has sacrificed the chance of getting to first for the sake of a teammate advancing.

THE ROLE OF A MANAGER

The baseball manager takes on the same job as a head coach in football, basketball, or hockey. Managers make many decisions during a game. A manager will decide who the starting pitcher will be, and when to bring in a reliever. Managers may visit the pitching mound during a game to talk about how the pitcher is feeling or discuss strategy.

Managers are experts on every aspect of the game. Many are ex-players. As well as coaching their team in games, managers run their team's practices and strategy sessions between games and during the off-season.

The manager always comes out to the mound to make a pitching change in pro baseball. The departing pitcher hands the manager the ball.

COACHES ON THE FIELD

Managers are assisted by many coaches on a team, and one of the most important is the pitching coach. This coach works with pitchers in practice to refine skills and build endurance. During a game, the pitching coach talks to the manager about how pitchers are doing, if they are still strong or getting tired, and if they may need to be taken out of the game and replaced with a reliever.

Pitching coaches may also visit the mound during a game to speak to a pitcher. Then, the discussion is often about how to pitch to a certain batter, or how to improve delivery and pitching mechanics. Most pitching coaches are former pitchers themselves.

THE BEST OF THE PITCHERS

The history of baseball is filled with great pitchers. Cy Young played 22 seasons in the major leagues between 1890 and 1911 and broke many pitching records. The annual awards for the best pitchers in the major leagues are named after him. Randy Johnson, known as the "Big Unit," stood a towering 6-foot-10 (2 m) and played in the majors between 1988 and 2009. He was known for an amazing fastball and won the Cy Young Award five times.

Greg Maddux (left) pitched for several teams, notably the Atlanta Braves, between 1986 and 2008. He is the only pitcher to win at least 15 games in a season for 17 straight seasons. Clayton Kershaw (right) of the Los Angeles Dodgers has won three Cy Young awards. He is one of the most dominating pitchers in MLB, though he was hampered by injury in 2016.

There are many great pitchers currently in Major League Baseball (MLB). Jake Arrieta of the Chicago Cubs won the National League Cy Young Award in 2015, and pitched a no-hitter the same season. Chris Sale broke into the majors with the Chicago White Sox in 2010. He has made five All-Star games and, in 2015, he led the American League in strikeouts.

Félix Hernández (left) of the Seattle Mariners is known as "King Félix " and pitched a perfect game in 2012—meaning he did not allow a single batter to reach first base. Noah Syndergaard (right) brings a blazing four-seam fastball that has been clocked at more than 100 mph (161 kph) to his games with the New York Mets. He is nicknamed Thor after the Norse god who hurls thunderbolts.

BE A GOOD SPORT

Playing to win is a big part of baseball. But fair play, good sportsmanship, and respect for the game are part of baseball's many traditions. Just as there are many rules that govern play on the field, the **unwritten rules** of the game, such as not gloating after hitting a home run or not stealing bases when your team has a big lead, go a long way to making baseball the great game it is. Even the pros know that being a good sport is key.

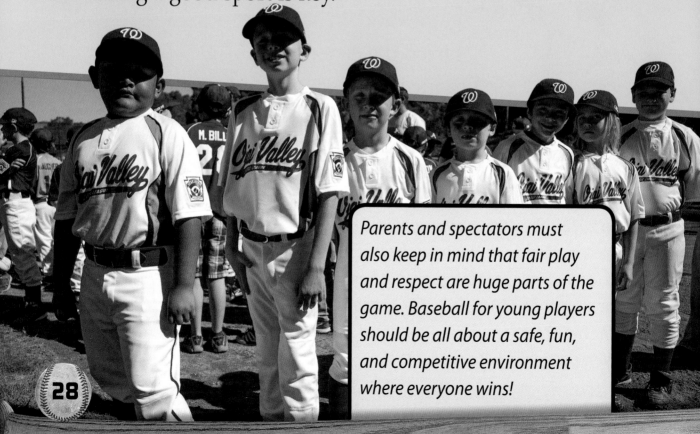

Parents and spectators must also keep in mind that fair play and respect are huge parts of the game. Baseball for young players should be all about a safe, fun, and competitive environment where everyone wins!

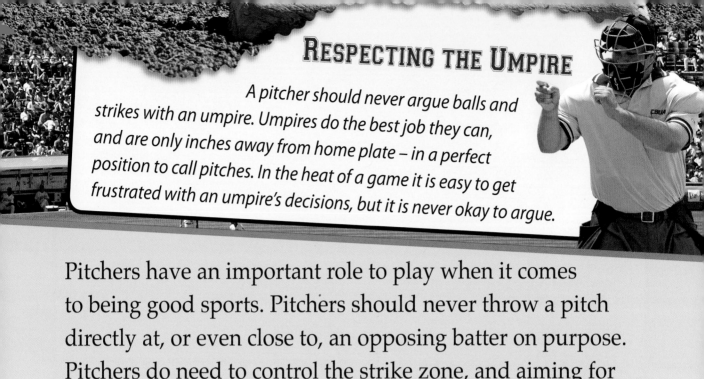

RESPECTING THE UMPIRE

A pitcher should never argue balls and strikes with an umpire. Umpires do the best job they can, and are only inches away from home plate – in a perfect position to call pitches. In the heat of a game it is easy to get frustrated with an umpire's decisions, but it is never okay to argue.

Pitchers have an important role to play when it comes to being good sports. Pitchers should never throw a pitch directly at, or even close to, an opposing batter on purpose. Pitchers do need to control the strike zone, and aiming for the inside of the plate is always acceptable. But throwing brush-back pitches, or trying to send a message by intentionally hitting a batter, are never acceptable in youth baseball.

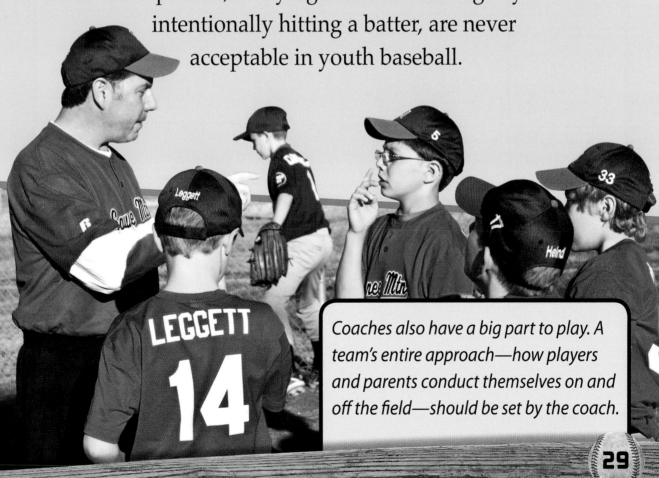

Coaches also have a big part to play. A team's entire approach—how players and parents conduct themselves on and off the field—should be set by the coach.

GLOSSARY

ace The baseball nickname given to the top pitcher on a team.

battery The two-player unit made up of the pitcher and the catcher.

bullpen The area within a baseball stadium where pitchers warm up.

closer A relief pitcher who specializes in getting the last outs of the game.

foul ball A baseball hit into the areas outside of the marked field of play.

mound The area of raised earth that pitchers throw the ball from.

pinch hitter A substitute who bats for the scheduled hitter. The replaced player cannot return to the game.

pitch selection The choice of pitches a pitcher makes during a game.

reliever A pitcher who comes into a game to replace a starting pitcher or another relief pitcher.

rotation The starting pitchers (usually 5) that a team uses over a period of time.

starter A pitcher who starts the game and is expected to pitch for several innings or even the whole game.

unwritten rules Unofficial practices that are generally followed, usually involving behavior.

FOR MORE INFORMATION

FURTHER READING

The Editors of Sports Illustrated Kids. *Baseball: Then to WOW!* New York: Sports Illustrated, 2016.

The Editors of Sports Illustrated Kids. *Sports Illustrated Kids Full Count*. New York: Sports Illustrated, 2012.

Graves, Will. *The Best MLB Pitchers of All Time*. Mankato, MN: Sportszone, 2014.

WEBSITES

Due to the changing nature of Internet links, PowerKids Press has developed an online list of websites related to the subject of this book. This site is updated regularly. Please use this link to access the list:

www.powerkidslinks.com/bs/pitcher

INDEX